Paradigm Books

TAPESTRY OF MYSTERY
Poetry Inspired by J. Krishnamurti

Dr. Somendra Pant was born in India on
June 23, 1954. He got his M.Sc. in Physics in
1976 (with distinction) and was selected as a
Probationary Officer in the State Bank of
India in 1978. In 1983 he joined the Rishi
Valley School of J. Krisshnamurti. Later, he
went to the US and got his MS and PhD
degrees from the Rensselaer Polytechnic
Institute in Troy, NY. He taught
Management Information Systems for 22
years as a Tenured Associate Professor at
Clarkson University in Potsdam, NY, where
he is now an Associate Professor Emeritus.

This book is my tribute to J. Krishnamurti,
who not only helped me unravel some of the
most profound mysteries of life, but in the
first place, also made me aware that life is a
rich tapestry of mystery.

Krishnamurti defies all description. He has
been variably called a Philosopher, Spiritual
Leader, World Teacher, Mystic, Sage, Writer,
Speaker, Incarnation of Christ, Buddha, etc.

Dr. Somendra Pant

Tapestry of Mystery

Paradigm Books

Paradigm Books is an imprint of Aldwych Associates.
2020 Pennsylvania Avenue NW, Ste 904
Washington DC 20006, USA
books@aldwychassociates.com

Made and printed in USA
Typeset in Century Schoolbook
Cover photograph © Gurpreet S. Dhillon

ISBN-13: 978-1-935160-22-9 (Paradigm Books)

Dedication

I dedicate this collection to Spiritual Teacher J. Krishnamurti; to Harish Pant, my father – a saint, a loving soul, a wonderful teacher, and above all, a great human being; to mystic poet, Kabir; to the poet of all poets, Mirza Ghalib; and to my best friend, Dr. Suman Agrawal, who, unfortunately, is not around to read this book.

Contents

Acknowledgements

I would like to thank my wife Saloni, mother Kiran, sister Mini, her husband Zach, late brother Pankaj, and innumerable friends, most notably, Rakesh, Nancy, Ingrid, Ellen, Gail, Dave, Santosh, Prakash, Lalit, Ratnesh, Suresh, Virendra, Mohan, and Harsh, who have been priceless companions in this wonderful journey and in providing the inspiration to write this book. Very special thanks to friends Paul Cannell, Prof. Joe Duemer, and Prof. Arthur H. Bell who motivated me to start writing again, and to Prof. Gurpreet Dhillon for his kind help in publishing this book.

This Book

This book is my tribute to J. Krishnamurti, who not only helped me unravel some of the most profound mysteries of life, but in the first place, also made me aware that life is a rich tapestry of mystery.

Krishnamurti defies all description. He has been variously called a Philosopher, Spiritual Leader, World Teacher, Mystic, Sage, Writer, Speaker, Incarnation of Christ, Buddha, etc.

Born on May 12, 1895, in Madanapalle, a small town in South India, Krishnamurti was "discovered" by Theosophist Charles Leadbeater as the coming World Teacher. Theosophist Annie Beasant adopted Krishnamurti (along with his younger brother Nitya) and took him to England where he was groomed to be the World Teacher. In 1911, an Order of the Star in East was created to prepare the world for the coming of the World Teacher. This Order became a powerful and rich organization and had followings all over the world. In a surprise move, in 1929, Krishnamurti made a famous speech in which he said: "I maintain that truth is a pathless land, and you cannot approach it by any path whatsoever, by any religion, by any sect", and dissolved the Order. For nearly 60 years after that, till his death on February 17, 1986, he travelled all over the world, giving talks, and holding large and small group discussions with people from all walks of life. In his own words, his mission was "to set man unconditionally free". He established a few schools in India, the US, and

England. Krishnamurti Foundations in various countries continue to support his work by publishing books, videos, and audio tapes.

When I was 23, I happened to pick one of his books: *Think About These Things* at a book store in New Delhi. Before that I had read a lot of Philosophy, both Eastern and Western, and Spiritual Writings of many. None of that really satisfied me. Reading that book was like finding all the answers. So, I read whatever Krishnamurti books I could lay my hands on. Someone lent me the audio tapes of his talks and listening to him speak was even more powerful than reading his books. In 1981, in Bombay (now Mumbai) for the first time I heard him speak in person. By then I had joined the State Bank of India as a Probationary Officer, which was one of the best jobs available in India then. In 1982 I had a chance to meet Krishnamurti in person. In 1983, I left my job and joined his school, Rishi Valley, in South India.

So, what did I learn from Krishnamurti? A lot. He changed my life like none other did.

During my brief meeting with him in 1982, I was a shy young man of 28. Hesitatingly I asked him: "Sir, what do you mean by Observer is the Observed?" He laughed and said: "Find out." It took me nearly 40 years to figure that out.

During one luncheon meeting with him at Rishi Valley, the discussion hovered around: "What will change man?" I used to dabble in writing poetry then, but was too shy to participate in the discussion. It is a mystery to me that he looked me directly in the eyes and asked: "Will poetry do it?" (meaning will poetry change man?). I didn't reply, but didn't write any poetry for the next 30 years. Only last year did I start writing again. Poetry will not change a person, but it surely is an effective medium of communicating one's inner thoughts and feelings, of unraveling the mysteries of life.

Over 50 of the poems in this collection are centered around the themes that Krishnamurti prompted me to explore: Meaning of Life, Awareness, Boredom, Pleasure, Greed, Materialism, Sex, Death, and Nature. The rest are my own literary dabbling.

1 AWARENESS

("Awareness, without any choice, of the ways of the mind,
which is the breeder of illusion, is the beginning of meditation"
– J. Krishnamurti)

Equanimeous in dark and glare
Shakyamuni said: "Be aware"

Be aware of thoughts shallow and deep
Pay attention to emotions
In waking hours and in sleep

You are a creature of habit
A captive of your thoughts
You think you are free but you are it

So if you are it
What can you do?
Not much - just watch, see through it

Sit erect in a room very quiet
Let them come and watch
Thoughts, emotions, desire

When watched, they lose their sting
May be for a moment
You see your true nature, the zeitgeist

Your true nature is not it:
The cacophony of desire
That put you in this dark pit

For a moment you will be free
Unborn, undying, unattached
Blue sky, the bird, utterly carefree

But desires run deep and far
The next moment will be
- how wonderful: forever

In this castle of wind and sand
There is no forever
Truth is but air in a closed hand

The more you seek
The less you find
- the eternal hide and seek

Things are as they are every bit
And so will always be
Bereft of seeking, you too are it

2 POETRY AND PROSE

"What will you do post-retirement" a friend asked
"I will write"
"Oh wow, what do you write?"
"Only two things"
"What are they?"
"Poetry and Prose"
The friend
 - smiled in poetry, laughed in prose

3 TRIBUTE TO POETRY

When the heart is torn
Poetry is born
After eyes weep dry
You can hear her cry
In a house deserted and ghostly
It wails by itself, oh so silently
A newborn cries in its verse
Tender soul, scared by a world stern
It runs with the workhorse feisty
Only to collapse, defeated and weary
It sits with the old lady
Brittle, tired, lost, and lonely
As an endnote you hear her dirge
 - meaningless complaining to ashes and dirt

4 WOMAN IN BLACK

Draped in black
She was poetry inflamed
Luminous black fire
Burning in dark recesses
Countenance ablaze
With a million dark devastating desires
Char me
O' timeless inferno

5 DUSKY DARK

What dark tales
Her dark eyes tell?

Who can tell?
For sure
The listener is under a spell

6 LIFE'S CURSES

All the life's curses
Have become my verses

My heart keeps bleeding
And keeps repeating
Impotent prayers and pleadings

He is on a long furlough
The all loving creator
- one who created this inferno

There were a few friends
But they too are out
On their own errands

Wine has turned to vinegar
Whiskey to sorrow yellow
Cheer of youth to deep despair

The cat has stopped meowing
The dog has stopped barking
And the bird is in deep mourning

Sun shines in somber luster
And the broken pallid moon
Awaits her own adjuster

Hill is sunk in to deep valley
And silly mountain
Stands like Nature's own folly

Not much else to say
This requiem is
A tribute to another bad hair day

7 ORPHANED

They used me
They abused me

Packed me up high
With their useless buy

They dragged me inside the store
They dragged me outside the store

Children rode me
With materialistic glee

Adults had stars in their eyes
Until bills arrived - oh, sighs

I carried cure for high cholesterol
Diabetes, heart burn, Pepto-Bismol

Sometime it was lingerie skimpy
Sometime jeans tattered 'n slinky

Never once did I complain
To these masters of inane

Now here I stand abandoned
A relic of greed wanton

8 CHATTER THAT MATTERED

These trees mattered
Birds here chattered

Trees are since long gone
In their place, the coffee house of the town

People here chatter
- chatter that doesn't matter

9 LITERARY-CULINARY

Poetry and Ballad
Soup and Salad

Liturgy and Canon
Eggs and Bacon

Fiction and Folklore
Stew and Casserole

Jokes and Banter
Bread and Butter

Story and Drama
Pinto and Lima

Sonnet and Ode
Jam and Toast

Memoirs and Diaries
Oats and Berries

Lyrics and Prose
Hotdogs and Sloppy Joes

Music and Lyric
Mustard and Garlic

Syllables and Rhythms
Honey and Almonds

Short Stories and Digests
Fries and Chicken Breasts

Verse and Stanza
Beer and Pizza

10 RAIN

Pitter-patter rain
Falls on the leaf
Earth feels relief
Clouds feel grief

11 UP AND DOWN

The Dow goes up the Dow goes down
Hopes go up hopes go down

From dawn to dusk from dusk to dawn
Heart goes up heart goes down

When the dust settles down
The epithet: "Weary warrior, out & down"

12 GREEN

For minutes twenty and thirteen
Poetry was lost in green –

Grass, shoots, leaves
Were all so green
Cosmos itself was green-serene

Quiet chameleon was green
The watchful snake
Watched it with eyes green

Green was the blue river
The omnipotent sky
Too gave a green shudder

The lass in orange jeans
Felt so embarrassed
- she wished it turned green

Birds sang a green song
Butterflies
Fluttered green wings for long

After minutes twenty and thirteen
The world stirred
And poetry was resurrected in green

13 SPAM STORY

Once upon a time
Spam was promises of good time:

Meet and date girls cute
Dance in the rain
Jump with a parachute

Prestigious and Ivy
Colleges beckoned on
With jobs great and sexy

Air travel, casinos, cruises
Bohemian delights
Booze, music jazz & blues

Chocolates soft and melty
Three toppings pizza
Beer fresh brewed and frosty

In phase two
Came in spam
With a different hue:

Hair transplant
Six pack abs
- all without a sweat

Eat all you can
Great foods
Still, no weight gain

Mortgage rates, oh so low
That six cylinder car
Was always in the tow

Phase three is not so fun
Spam get nasty
Brutal, direct, without pun:

Viagra without prescription
Adult diapers
To negotiate incontinence

Right Part B supplement
To Medicare
Is every retiree's predicament

Your house you sell
Get reverse mortgage
In that nursing home you settle

Cruelty alas doesn't stop at that
- hey, get burial insurance
Before it is too late!

14 LE MISERABLE

Being childless for long
For a child she longed

She was miserable

To many clinics she went
Pleaded to Gods
Pitifully, diligently, no end

She was miserable

Gods took pity, petition was granted
She was blessed with a child
Just as she so badly wanted

Oh, she was happy!

It was a cute healthy boy
Center of her universe
Circumference of her joy

Oh, she was happy!

The boy didn't do too well at school
Army of tutors came
Work, work, work, but to no avail

She was miserable

With great difficulty a job he got
Not what mommy wanted
But then not all get the top slot

She was miserable

In due course he got a bride
Not as hot as neighbor's
And again was bruised her pride

She was miserable

The boy loved the wife alright
Fun and frolic
Away he went, mom was torn apart

She was miserable

She now sits with an album rusty
Often brushing memories
Far away, faded, and dusty

She is miserable

To Gods she again petitions
Pitifully, diligently, no end
- please, forever, end my contrition

She is miserable

15 DEATH

It is a process, not an event
Everything dies every moment

He doesn't step in the river twice
- good old Heraclitus
For with first step, he too dies

Flowers die, die stars bright
Craving immortality
Is so meaningless, so futile

Seven years is all it takes
For all body cells to die
- in 63 years, 9 lives body rakes

Flowers bloom and die in glory
Poor humans
Meet an end so ugly and gory

Scary not is death itself
But the thought
That it will be the final farewell

Farewell to all the riches
To heady wine
To a million cherished wishes

But inevitable is it to die
- go out kicking
Or peacefully, with a smile

Those who court this damsel coy
Live life fully
Bow out with a cheerful goodbye

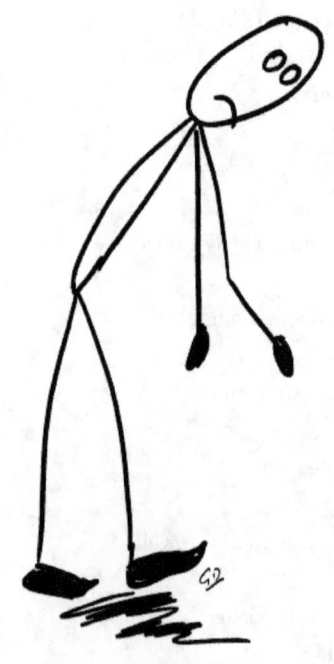

16 TIRED OLD MAN

Tired old man
Craved sex, fun, game

Youth was wasted in taboo
Fire tamed
By moralistic "don't do"

For years on end
He struggled
To meet ends

More mouths to feed
Children arrived
Creatures of want and greed

Parents grew old and tired
That too
Doused the dying fire

World went steadily distant
A life wasted calculating
Pension, gratuity, fund provident

In the end there was fire
It burnt for a day:
Ashes, requiem, end of desire

17 MARRIED

Back home
No back in home
 - status: Married

18 MEANINGLESS DAY

Roosters crow
Hens lay
- yet another meaningless day

19 THE POWER OF NO

Eckhart is famous for NOW
I muse on the Power of NO

Say NO to them all
Drinks, drugs, nicotine
To that junk food stall

Say NO to the preacher, to the crowd
Be your own savior
Of your own counsel be proud

Say NO to parents unreasonable
To tired old teachers
To the trendy who are merely seasonal

Say NO to that friend
Who in his misery unending
On you forever depends

Have courage to say NO to spouse
Dull, dry, dour
One who is always morose

Say NO to them kids
Who forever want more
This, that, other, everything

Say NO to work that never ends
To that sadist boss
Who never bends

Say NO to commercials on TV
To spam in the inbox
To the lure of life sexy

You don't owe anyone anything
Your life is your own
How you write it, how it you sing

The more you practice NO
The more will yours be peace
More the energy to your own way go

20 SOME DAY

Someday the wind will turn
Someday happy days will come

Darkness may be so full of fright
Howsoever long
Night still succumbs to dawn's light

Someday to shores familiar will it sail
- the ship broken and leaky
Someday the seabird will rest on mast frail

Someday the cuckoo will sing a song old
Someday the caged peacock
Will again dance its dance bold

Someday little less will ache the heart
Someday the weary soul
Will find some respite in its journey tart

Don't lose heart says a squeaky voice:
When all is lost, hope burns bright
Gods grant happiness – often as the last choice

21 ISLANDS

No man is an island
But some are gems of the land

John at 8 AM drinks to his health
Has lost it all
His wife, kids, will, wealth

Jack, a chronic gambler
Sold his house
- now sleeps in a shelter

Joshua is the author of two felonies
Three misdemeanors
Has lost count of his petty larcenies

Jane, so beautiful then
Has drug addiction
She now walks the streets at ten

Joe searched for enlightenment
To India he went
- mumbo jumbo is his sole entitlement

Jeannie, bless her, was born twice
Two miscarriages
Four boyfriends, been divorced thrice

I tell you brother forever and anon
Without their sacrifices
Others wouldn't qualify as oh, so normal

22 CEMETERY

The best place to walk is
Where all are peaceful

After arguing for years forty-seven
The Smiths are peaceful
Here, and in heaven

Brown always envied Bill's house's view
Bill now overlooks the river
Brown is happy with his abode under the yew

John was ever so loud
Jack, oh, ever so perturbed
Both now silently watch the drifting cloud

Mary always had a resentful eye
On Megan's bosom, on her pendant
Serenely now they lay side by side

Rich was oh so rich 'n profligate
Paul, the pauper tight
No more McDonald's for him, for him no more steak

Susan forever struggled with her girth
Sandy's hour glass figure had heads turned
Now they both laugh with uncontrolled mirth

Philip aced all his classes
Peter petered out of school high
RIP the duo under tall grasses

If peace was theirs to be had while alive
They would have all lived it then
Instead of living it in this afterlife

23 CEMETERY REVISITED

Best place in the town to be
Is this serene cemetery

No one does anyone fight
None from his pocket
Pulls out a Bill of Rights

No one is black or white
Or a shade of gray
- everyone is just right

No foot soldiers here nor knights
All are enjoying
Their well-deserved night

Nowhere to go, no hurry, no rush
All have rested
In Spring's salubrious blush

No agonizing over one's gender
All are happy
Straight, gay, bisexual, transgender

None is rich nor poor
All houses have
Open windows, open door

Thank you Lord for granting them peace
I'll praise you again
When you stitch my torn heart in one piece

24 HER OWN WEIGHT

She is so fat
Weighed down by her own weight

At one time skinny she was
Bubbly, sprightly
Youth of spring, unlimited grace

She jumped, sang, danced
With gay abandon
Delight to herself and to all who glanced

So, what happened, what went wrong?
Where did the spring go
When was lost that dance, that song?

She was weighed down by stress her own
She put that weight on herself
Bite by bite, ice cream cone by cone

Boredom was yet another factor
Constant ennui
Made her reach for that juicy steak

If she wasn't so lonesome
She would have avoided
Munching on snacks unwholesome

Now at age 50 and sundry
She is scheduled for
Bariatric surgery

Her tummy will be short circuited
Food will pass through her
But will not be much absorbed

All this was so unnecessary
- if she had short circuited her cravings
Healthy she would be without surgery

25 OMAD

One meal a day
Makes my day

In bad old days

Food was stored
I ate when bored

The scale went North
There was only sloth

Now in my old clothes I glow
Bounce up and down like a doe

One has to be quite MAD
To not to do OMAD

26 LITTLE MISS MUFFET

Little Miss Muffet
Sat on a tuffet,
Eating her curds and whey;
Along came a spider
Who sat down beside her
Reminded her of her lactose intolerance
And frightened Miss Muffet away

27 LITTLE JACK HORNER

Little Jack Horner
Sat in the corner,
Eating his pity pie;
He twiddled his thumb,
And was so glum,
And said, "What a sad boy am I"

28 HUMPTY DUMPTY

Humpty Dumpty sat on street called Wall,
Humpty Dumpty had a great fall.
All the king's financiers and all the king's bankers
Couldn't put Humpty's portfolio together again.

29 SANDWICH

Two cute witches
Shared one sandwich

One witch got sand
One witch got wich

Which witch got sand
Which witch got wich?

PS. Sandy got sand
The other left the stand
(I didn't get her name)

30 NO REASON, ONLY RHYME

One two
How do I do?

Three four
I am a bore

Five six
Is there a fix?

Seven eight
Learn to wait

Nine ten
Egg lays the hen

31 DESTINY

Children of Destiny
That is who we are
Know not whence we came
Nor where we go

Two semi-anonymous people
Who our bills pay

Where are they now?
Or will be, one day

Not a single breath is our own
Nor a single heart beat
Not a murmur we make
Nor write a single sheet

Children of Destiny
That is who we are

Some time we think
That we are in control

And order pizza
With extra cheese
Or
Wine with cheese

Someday soon
There is no pizza, no wine
No nothing
Nary anything to whine

And then Mom Destiny
Gently lulls us to sleep

Children of Destiny
That is who we were

32 ANONYMOUS

To drink
Or not to drink
Is the question

I drink
Therefore I am
Charming, witty, sexy

I drink
Therefore I am
Boisterous, obnoxious, perilous

So back to the basic:
To drink
Or not to drink

33 LOVE THYSELF

Finally, I love myself

For long
I fought myself

Was too fat
Was too flat

Ate too much
Drank too much

Watched too much porn
Had too much scorn

Nothing was right
Heart was trite

Wife nagged
Belly sagged

Gym was a chore
Mirror was a bore

But finally
I love myself

Oh dear ..

34 ALL OK

Nothing much to write
I guess that is OK
Nothing much to fight
I guess that is OK

Nothing much to say
I guess that is OK
No bills to pay
I guess that is OK

No activity
I guess that is OK

No inactivity
I guess that is OK

Health is OK
I guess that is OK
Wealth is OK
I guess that is OK

Lot of snow
I guess that is OK
Wrinkles on the brow
I guess that is OK

The old lady is old
I guess that is OK
The young lady is young
I guess that is OK

Some have jobs
I guess that is OK
Some don't have jobs
I guess that is OK

Some are dead
I guess that is OK
Some are not dead
I guess that is OK

The rooster crows
I guess that is OK
The cow doesn't crow
I guess that is OK

I am bored
I guess that is OK
This is a terrible poem
I guess that is OK

35 TWO BY TWO

Two cats
Don't make a dog
But two dogs
Make a lot of noise

Two pans
Don't make an omelet
But two omelets
Make a lot of breakfast

Two heads
Don't make a body
But two bodies
Make a lot of fight

Two scores
Don't make a hundred
But two hundreds
Make a lot of change

Two idiots
Don't make anything
But two anything's
Make a lot of something's

Two bicycles
Don't make a car
But two cars
Make a lot of dents

Two bells
Don't make a church
But two churches
Make a lot of baloney

Two walls
Don't make a room
But two rooms
Make a lot of room

Two buds
Don't make a rose
But two roses
Make a lot of romance

Two kids
Don't make an Indian
But two Indians
Make a lot of kids

Two drops
Don't make a shot
But two shots
Make a lot of evening

36 FIREWORKS

A lone star
Fires up the moon
Back home: Only fireworks

37 KIN LOVE

Yesterday there was a fight at the fraternity
Today, the sorority is catty

38 SNOW WHITE

Poor Snow White
Is no longer so white

She moved to a city
In a factory she works
Is covered with soot, oh pity

The gallant prince, her rescuer
Drives the FedEx truck
Drinks beer, is a chronic curser

Four kids they have
Two boys, two girls
All Facebook and Twitter slave

Who sent her in exile, the old hag
She remarried a rich guy
Now has a smart mirror with truth lag

But hey, without happily ever after
No fairy tale ends
Whitening cream she won for ever and after

39 LIFE

("It's a tale told by an idiot, full of sound and fury, signifying nothing" – Shakespeare)

It's a journey
From nowhere to nowhere

Many go out painting the town red
Those bored beings
Who only the outer world tread

They get married, bells chime
Divorce lawyers smile
And wait for their time

Children arrive in due time
Bills mount
Everyone works, no time

McDonald's, Burgers, Pizza
Chocked arteries
Life is no longer a happy piazza

Kids work overtime to succeed
Parents worry endlessly
No one really succeeds

In pensive moments they muse
Those wasted beings
And ask, "What was the use"?

Mercifully bells do chime
Epithet:
"Here lies one sans reason or rhyme"

End of the story.

40 SIMPLICITY

The best city to live in
Is simplicity

Simple foods
Are the healthiest food

Simple thoughts
Are the deepest thoughts

A simple home is uncluttered
A simple person is most cultured

Simple words are never cheap
Simple acts big rewards reap

A simple honest smile
Never tires, traverses a mile

A simple toy fires beautiful imagination
A simple prayer is a profound supplication

A simple song touches hearts
A simple tune never departs

Simple acts fetch results deep
Simple minds need least upkeep

Wasn't it rightly said:

Blessed are the simple at heart
For they alone will meet the Lord

41 THE WALL

The good old wall
Was etched with them all:

He was there - Johnny
So was Toni
Not far behind was Ronny

With a bleeding heart
Samantha loved Sam
Susie too was no pop tart

Many dates heralded
Their arrivals heroic
Some are fresh, some faded

They came, they etched
They left
Travelers in time stretched

The wall stood firm
With a resolve so stoic
- but was dust at the end of its term

42 STUFF DREAMS ARE MADE OF

(This was an actual ad)

For sale
A wedding ring
Never worn
$ 250
Or best offer

43 BUSY

Busy busy busy
The bee is busy
The busy busy busy bee
Is busy with glee

Busy busy busy
I am busy
The busy busy busy me
Is dying prematurely

44 ARROW OF TIME

The arrow of time
Hits its target every time

It hits the humble and low
High and mighty
Feisty and fighty also go

Some go comatose
Some kicking and screaming
But go all, fine and gross

No one knows whence it came
Or where it goes
It is its own glory, acclaim

A child is carried in its lap
An invalid sleeps in its arms
The unborn too is in its trap

Some think it is their foe
Some, their friend
To none is it friend or foe

Sometime it moves quiet as a damsel coy
With unabashed fury at other time
But it moves always, grief or joy

The ignorant and the astute wonder:
Why does it every time its target hit?
"Whatever it hits is the target" is my answer

45 DARKNESS

("One does not become enlightened by imagining figures of
light, but by making the darkness conscious" - Carl Jung)

Darkness in me
Burns bright

Despair looms large
Fear is foreboding
Hopelessness is in full charge

To be born is to be in pain
Occasional bouts of mirth
Accentuate existence vain

Heart is a bundle of ache
Mind, a whirligig
Soul, forever bleak and black

Gods committed hara-kiri
Angels are in deep slumber
Devil dances it's dance scary

Whoever thought sunshine
Hadn't had a tryst with dark clouds
- all dreams of drunkard moonshine

Life in its essence is a chore
Meaningless syllables
Uttered by an imbecile bore

Thereby hangs a wasted story
Utterly impotent, futile
Dull, decadent, dreary

46 RIVER

Bend in the river
Does not end the river

Poetry is it?
It flows in canto and canon
Melody new forever and anon

Music is it?
It sings in spates so high
Sometime it is just a faint sigh

Friend is it?
It blesses lovers in matrimony
It consoles souls solitary

Arbitrator is it?
Newborns are christened at its shores
It carries ashes to distant shores

Life is it?
It is home to lives many
In its fury it is death scary

Mother is it?
On its bosom a new day dawns
In its lap a tired evening yawns

Mystery is it?
Where it came from where it goes
Many wonder, write poetry, no one knows

47 RIVER TODAY

Why, I fail to understand
River today did a crazy headstand

Trees grew tall upside down
Two confused ducks
Swam together in one bridal gown

A seagull soared high up in water
Kissed its mirror mate
And the two were one thereafter

A leaf, withered and brown
Rose up to the surface
And floated away from the town

Tired sun oh so sulky yellow
Emerged from one end
And soon vanished the odd fellow

Proud Church too was not the same
In mournful confession
It hung its head in shame

The kayak blue and red
Drifted upside down
- an idiot on a fool's errand

Today I think bad was river's hair
Let it sleep tonight
Tomorrow it will be fine for sure

48 LOVE LETTERS

To the river
Trees sent a million love letters
- the river was not interested

49 RIVER AGAIN

Yesterday the river was quiet
Melancholy and remote
Today, wind will not leave it alone

50 THE DUCK

Waves toss the duck
The duck ducks
- and becomes the wave

51 RIVER AT NIGHT

River at night -
Her own groom
His own bride

52 BLUSH

The river was deep blue
Kissed by the setting sun
It blushed in many hues

53 FALLEN WARRIOR

Knocked down by wind
This fallen warrior
Is still glorious in defeat

54 LOVE

Love drops like rain
A bird chirps
In the distance, a train

55 NOWHERE

To be near is to be distant
To be distant is to be near
To be in the middle is to be nowhere

56 LOST AND FOUND

He who seeks, finds
He who finds, loses
He who either finds or loses
Neither finds nor loses

57 I AM ME

I am
My pain
My pleasure
My sorrow
My anxiety
My anger
My hope
My despair
My moodiness
My gloominess
...
Ad infinitum

The more
I fight myself
The stronger
I become
More energy
To fight myself
More confusion
More despair

Is not fighting myself
An option at all?

58 SHE

She walked a weary walk
She talked a weary talk

A zillion lines did her face crisscross
Happiness nailed to many a cross

Her eyes vacant and distant
Looked for hope non existent

To hope is to live
When hope dies, what lives?

A heart so laden
With beats mournful and uneven

It fell and sank like them waves
- ocean rough and untamed

With a deep sigh she complained
To Gods to pedestals chained

But Gods neither listen nor talk
- moot spectators to a world in shock

And that's how life itself lived
Meaningless, empty, broken, unenvied

59 BATTLE ROYAL

You beat me
I beat you

You beat me till I am bruised
I beat you till you are bruised

You beat me till you are bruised
I beat you till I am bruised

Why do you beat me?
Why do I beat you?

Deep down you are broken
Deep down I am broken

Your pain is lessened when I am hurt
My pain is lessened when you are hurt

Your pain is lessened when you are hurt
My pain is lessened when I am hurt

We fight till we bleed, hurt, are sore
Oblivious that the pain was actually in the soul

60 CORPSE

(This is a translation of a Hindi poem)

On a solitary road
I met a corpse

He had freshly arisen from the grave
- unkempt hair, blank eyes, soiled shroud

We walked in silence for a while

Then he stopped
Took my hand in his icy hands
And said: "How unfortunate that you are still alive"

I said: "True, I am still scared of death"

61 PROSE Vs. POETRY

Prose is prosaic
Poetry is poetic

Prose is boring 'n long
Poetry is a sweet song

Prose meanders like a drunk walk
Poetry goes straight to the heart

In prose we fight like fools
In poetry we love and drool

Prose is an idiot's apology
Poetry is wisdom's eulogy

Mundane is written in prose
Poetry smiles in wine and rose

With due apologies to Puritans:
To prose's bitter feuding sarcasm
Poetry is ecstatic lovers' orgasm

62 SPRING

Two trees
Two cars
Spring in the air too

63 SITTING QUIETLY

("Sitting quietly, doing nothing, spring comes and grass grows
by itself" - Zen saying.)

The world is undone
By too much doing

Mindless running
From nowhere to nowhere
Mindless chattering
About everything, everywhere

The restless soul wanders
To temples, mosques, churches
Forever it looks for peace
In holy places, in wise discourses

To the agitated traveler
Soothsayers say words soothing
Many a talisman, charms
Help not fears deep and foreboding

Pleadings, pilgrimages, prostrations
Endless praying to Gods nonexistent
All anemic attempts
At assuaging the pain deep 'n persistent

Only if the scared traveler
Had paused in his search vain
And looked within
He would have found a cure for his pain

For he is the pain that
Pervades his tortured soul
He is it
-the pain and its author sole

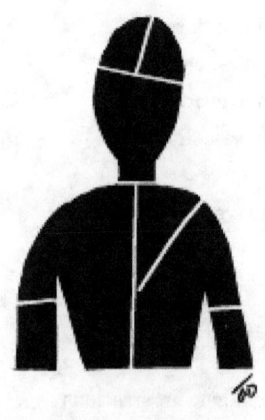

64 STORY OF AN HOUR REVISITED

(Inspired by Kate Chopin's 1894 masterpiece)

A dead spouse
Is the best spouse

It doesn't speak
Nags it not
- an open door that doesn't squeak

With a spouse oh so dead
There are no quarrels
Such a beauty is it on the shelf

In half are cut the bills to be paid
Doubled is the joy
Of leisurely mornings uncontested

Every vacation is your own
Every movie
Every song stirs your soul

No one competes for kids' love
They embrace you tight
Knowing well that only you are left

No more mother-brother-sister in laws
Be as lawless as you wish
For once you are without all those flaws

Usually a new romance it begets
Love-you cards, roses
Wine, hugs, kisses, not-me-forgets

So my dear friends let me tell you
If your spouse kicks the bucket
Smile, look up, and say: "Thank You"

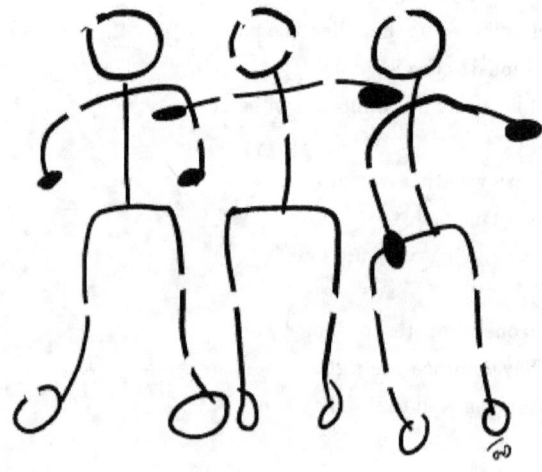

65 SEVEN BORED GHOSTS

Seven bored ghosts
Set out to have fun

One went to the bar
Slipped under the counter
Drank all the wine in the jar
What fun he had!

One went to the casino
Made machines go haywire
Made a ton of dough
What fun he had!

One went to the golf course
Carried balls to the holes
Won the contest, applause
What fun he had!

One went to the forbidden street
Sat on the dude's shoulder
To the lady in bed sang songs sweet
What fun he had!

One went to a wedding
Walked up the aisle
Said "I do" before the groom was ready
What fun he had!

One went to a race course
Scared away six horses

His horse alone ran the course
What fun he had!

One, the lazy one, stayed back
While other ghosts were out
He ate all their bacon and steak
What fun he had!

66 ADIEU

In your sham earnestness
You were oh so earnest

One sincere word
I waited to get from you
All that I got were words

Words from mind's vault
Carefully crafted
Not a single syllable from the heart

For you knew too well
That heart doesn't lie
- lies alone you needed to tell

I don't blame you
For being who you are
- you like me are the morning's dew

Life is bigger than us mortals
It sings and dances
To its own cries, to its own chortles

Always a dark dusky mystery
Life is forever new
No one fathoms it, gullible or astute

So in this journey of an hour
Stranger, I wish you well
Let's bid adieu without being bitter or dour

67 MIGHTY DUCKS

Mighty ducks of the town
Care not for a smile or a frown

Forever and anon
They live by their own canon

If you get too close on
They are ready to take you on

Leave them alone
And they swim for long

68 THE SUPERSTORE

The town superstore
From all vantage is an eyesore

Brown and gray on a lot so big
It stands as a monument
Of human ignorance, greed, avarice

This section called bread
Is full of carbs
That should be everyone's dread

Move forward, there are oils refined
Heart aches, heart burns
Put there by conspirators so well aligned

The sweets section is not so sweet
Cakes, desserts, ice creams
"Diabetes" is what it should tweet

Clothes section is truly a scream
Of skimpy nymphs
Selling a very distant dream

'Exercise equipment' is deserted
Who has the time
In a life oh so well-orchestrated?

The guns section does boom
With murderous beings
So ready to kill a goose or a goon

The only honest section is pharmacy
It has a cure for all -
Obesity, diabetes, heartburn, melancholy

69 FUNERAL

Amidst flowers in baskets
Friend's son laid in a casket

On his face played a gentle smile
Of end of pain and strife

Parents with eyes red
Had run out of tears to shed

Did they cry for the boy
Or for the loss of their own joy?

Hard to say, mysterious is the heart
It keeps beating though torn apart

Hope burns bright in a lamp
That has burnt the oil, the wick, the lamp

In a pensive mood
Did I brood:

Living, if we can have the smile of the boy gone
Death will smile with us in an eternal dawn

70 DEATH OF A GODMAN

He was rich, powerful, good looking
 - Adonis in the house neighboring

His serene smile was oh so serene
Years of practice
To smile like sages, like Rasputin

His words came from oh what depth
Punctuate by silence
That mocked life, even death

"God's will be done, don't despair
Have faith, smile"
Was his constant refrain

Under his flag he did arrange
A lot of good
 - hospitals, kitchens, orphanage

They flocked to him like bees to a flower
Endless was his erudition
Unending the supply of divine nectar

He had everything they wished they had
- riches, power, good looks, wisdom
Alas, yesterday he shot himself in the head

71 SNOW IN MID-APRIL

Snow in mid-April
Spells peril

Bike is stowed
Jogging shoes are still
Even the squirrel is bored

Trees sigh in despair
Flawed look flowers
Buds need serious repair

Folks walk gingerly
Cursing under their breath
The sky still pours aimlessly

Birds are home
Muted are kids
The rabbit is in a snowy dome

Whoever ordained this snow
Sure had a contract
With the man with the plow

But hey, look at the side bright
Dismal as it is
It still is a poet's delight!

72 OF COURSE YOU

Mirror, mirror on the wall
Who is the prettiest of them all?

"Of course you"

Mirror, mirror on the wall
Who is the ugliest of them all?

"Of course everyone that's not you"

Mirror, mirror on the wall
Who are you?

"Oh, just your faithful ego"

73 FLIGHT 119

1A is flying South
3C, Southwest

3A will attend a funeral
5C, christening

5A, graduation
7C, son's bail

7A has a rosary in his hand
9C pulled a trigger yesterday

11A is rich and will die at 40
13C is broke and will live to be 90

13A has high libido
15C .. oh, well ..

15A lost big at the races
17C rode them all

17A is divorced
19C wishes that he was

If this flight crashed
Nothing will change

Some 1A will still fly South
Some 2C, Southwest

74 SCHRODINGER'S CAT REVISITED

This time around
Schrodinger put in the box a rat and a cat

Three different gases the box had
One would kill the cat
Second would kill the rat
Third would kill both the cat and the rat

If both lived
Then the cat would kill the rat

So, at the end of the experiment
What happened to the cat, to the rat?

Hard to say:
Only if died the cat
Would live the rat

But the cat has to die a lonely death

If the cat dies and along takes the rat
Then, obviously dies the rat

If the rat lives and dies the cat
Then does the poor creature live, the rat?

Not necessarily because the cat is only once dead
And further, there still are two gases

That can take out
The dead cat and the living rat

Which begs the question:
How can it live, or die, a cat dead?
Oh, because nine lives it had

75 EINSTEIN MUSED

Einstein looked at the stars for long
And said: "May he RIP, Newton was wrong"

Black holes don't fall at thirty two
Only red apples in Cambridge do

Nothing is constant - Newton's moustache
Grew wild when he had no cash

Wish he had travelled in my trains
Not on tired horses under strain

Horses sure can run, gallop, and canter
But my trains would have taught that chronic ranter

That light doesn't travel to a horse's behind
So what came out had to be asinine

He was a true genius old boy Watts
Made trains possible, put Newton in a spot

76 BIRD IN FLIGHT

A bird in flight
Is sky's glory, sky's delight

It soars so high
To dive down again
- her way of teasing the sky

Against the backdrop so blue
The white bird
Is an Angle's apparition so true

Sometimes she shrieks with joy
Sometimes with her head down
She sits like a bride so coy

Often she floats on the river serene
Serenity doubled
In a world so chaotic, cruel, mean

Wish she had seen the man with the gun
All that is left of her now
Are feathers, and blood that slowly runs

77 HELPLINE

At this end of the helpline
There was only helplessness

At the other end of the line
Was a paycheck
A spouse, a child, a pet feline

This end was distraught and dusty
Sans prayers, sans hope
Dismal, devastated, oh so ugly

This end was at the very end
Of any aye
All was lost, nothing left to mend

So, how do the twain talk
- hopelessness and hope
The two ends of a line-to-talk?

Well they don't really talk
Through a worksheet
They walk their mundane walk

"Take a deep breath, all will be fine"
Oh yeah
What is left to be fine?

Be courageous, be brave
The clouds shall pass
No night is without an end

Epilogue:
Fire burns long and bright
- when all is all lost
Fire that extinguishes all plight

78 STRANGE

Two strangers
Come together
Say: "I do"
Do strange things together
Remain strangers, together

79 BLACK BRA

His explanations are so fake
About a bra oh so black

One: Old tenant left it back
That insidious
Bra black

Two: It came in with laundry
The black bra
Is someone else's property

Three: May be it is your own
But the difference betwixt

38 and 34 is so out of tune

Mystery remains so bleak
About, yes,
That bra black

80 MOTHER

She who was our mainstay
Is now slipping away

For years close to seventy
She kept the fires burning
For us and the sundry

Her care is unbound
Her kindness
Makes Angels astound

She is love in person
Heart overflowing
With kindness in every season

Will I be sad when she travels far?
Hard to say
She belongs with Them in stars

81 PAIN

("To live is to live in pain" - Buddha)

In the middle of the night
Every night
My soul gets into a deadly fight

It fights a hundred demons scary
Masked faces
Ghoulish apparitions, twisted 'n eerie

Voices call in rising crescendo
Beckoning me on
To the netherworld of dark inferno

Transfixed to this bleeding cross
Often I am too scared
Senses numbed, subtle 'n gross

In anguish long and deep
I reach out to Him
One who is in a drunkard sleep

No mother, father, sibling
Friend or foe
This is soul's lone battle unending

Born was it to suffer in many hues
- all shades of dark
To pay for its sins long overdue

To the dreamy deluded Sunday preacher
I say:
Come lie here - thou shalt be a better teacher

82 THE FAWN

I asked her: "Your name, O' fawn"?
She said: "Dawn"

"How long will you graze, Dawn?"
"Oh, till dawn", said the fawn

"You are quite a glutton"
"'Because I eat no meat or mutton"

Quite a smart fawn
Was that supple Dawn!

83 CHIPPED TOOTH

She chipped her tooth
In a phone booth

There was no response
- oh so disconcerting
She bit hard into the phone cord

Out came a chip of the tooth
- other 31 are intact
Healthy, beautiful, faithful

So why should she worry about it
One chipped tooth
That shows not in a smile beatific?

But strange are women's ways
They can anguish over anything
- rooster that crows, hen that lays

I guess that tooth chipped
Will continue to sing
Its song in pathos deep

This poet idly muses:
May women grow teeth
Like nails, like tresses

84 AUGHT AND NAUGHT

When aught was aught
And naught, naught
What was, and what was not?

When aught was not aught
And naught, not naught
What was not was, and what was was not?

When aught was naught
And naught, aught
What was was not, and what not was was?

85 SILENCE

Silence crawls in
Like a coy bride
And embraces us
From side to side

It speaks not a word
But smiles a shy smile
Looks gently at us
For a second or a while

Do not ask it a thing
Let it quietly linger
It has a fragrance
That grows stronger

When left alone
It quietly tell us a lot
Who we are
- also, who we are not

We are not this cacophony
Not this drama, this malady
Nor this ominous dark cloud
That hangs there oh so steady

So, who we really are?
If we have the patience
We will eventually discover
- we ourselves are that silence

www.ingramcontent.com/pod-product-compliance
Lightning Source LLC
Chambersburg PA
CBHW070459130626
46555CB00003B/1081